ORGANIC GARDENING

WHAT IS ORGANIC GARDENING?

Originally, organic gardening was understood as good old natural gardening where you put the plants in the ground and let "mother nature" take over, while you sat back and watched your garden grown.

Today, organic gardening has become known by many titles including chemical-free gardening, earth-friendly gardening, and organic, but the reality of it is that although we use the term "chemical free" to mean "Organic", but that only applies if you use no fertil-izers or pesticides when creating and growing your garden.

So, basically, organic gardening requires it to be done naturally without the use of fertilizers and pesticides, which means that before you start your organic garden, you need to understand a few of the essential elements that will affect your gardens growth.

ESSENTIALLY, organic gardening consists of understanding the following three principles:

1. The Soil – Gardens require fertile soil to grow good crops;

therefore the richer you can make it, the better your organic garden will be.

2. Simplicity – One of the hardest things for most gardeners to do is let nature do its thing, but when organic gardening simple practices without chemical intervention work best.

3. Preventative Methods and Measures – Understanding the pros and cons of the pests that inhabit our gardens and how to rid them naturally and prevent them from arriving initially is a big part of organic farming and gardening.

2

___

CREATING PRODUCTIVE SOIL

With rich nutrient soil our gardens will produce bumper crops, so understanding how to maintain the soil and keep it so it is growing becomes a major consideration before you even plot your garden's layout. In today's society, where people have a tendency to deplete everything they touch, the land is not different. Every year, the earth losses layers of soil due to wind erosion, run off, and other more destructive building practices, and each year millions of acres of fertile land are consumed by man for building and expending cities, leaving very little workable land to feed the multitude.

With this being said, no matter what condition your soil is in, when using the organic method to gardening, it is recommended that you build your soil into a deep, dark, rich soil that can support and sustain a summer growing season. To do this, your entire garden will need to have a good base to grow in, so the more compost and organic manure, chopped leaves and natural mulches you can work into the soil before planting season, the better your garden will grow. Turning the soil over and over to aerate it is also a good practice. Crops like crumbly soil that is not packed hard.

Once your soil has been prepared, you can then set about to plan how you would like to lay your garden out, remembering to keep in mind that you want to take in the growing condition of each fruit or vegetable so that they receive as many of the natural elements as they require. For instance: If you have tomatoes growing that require lots of sunlight and water to grow, you would most likely be wise not to plant it next to corn that has a tendency to grow tall creating lots of shade, and drink in all the water available in its general area.

LAYOUT FOR A PRODUCTIVE GARDEN

When planning your organic garden there are many things you can do to produce the most yield. Many of these things are simple, although they do require some advance planning and generally, a little forethought when it comes to managing how the plants will work best depending on direction of sun, etc.

It is advisable to seek professional advice like for example a land-scaper. Walk through the garden and ask advice to find out which areas in the garden are suitable for vegetables, flowers, herbs, trees etcetera. The other option that you can try before investing your money in a landscaper is to visit your local nursery. The staff will be able to give you valuable information on what plants flourish in the area and the seasons that are the most suitable for the different types of vegetables and plants.

Start planning the garden according to the data you gather along the way. Make sure the area you choose for the vegetable garden is not too big and easy to maintain. Also opt for pathways between the various types of vegetables to prevent people from harming the crops. Place sheets of plastic underneath the pathway to stop weeds from growing. Plant the taller crops at the back of the vegetable garden and the herbs in between the different types of vegetables

If your space is limited use containers to plant your herbs and vegetables in. Remember that herbs act as a natural pesticide. It is wise to plant herbs throughout your garden. After you planned the layout of the organic garden walk through the garden again to make sure it is viable. Also be flexible some layouts look great on paper; but they are not practical. If you need more guidance use the Internet, garden magazines, public gardens and catalogs as a source to find layout concepts.

4

BENEFITS OF ORGANIC GARDENING

Not many people are aware that the benefits of organic gardening can improve their health, lifestyle and the envi-ronment. It is important that you understand what you can get out of the organic gardening process to reap the benefits.

- Growing your own vegetables can save you a lot of money. You can pick fresh vegetables from your own backyard. There is no need driving to the shop anymore, using fuel and money to buy lettuce, cucumber etcetera. Another plus is that due to the fact the herbs, fruit, vegetables are not treated with harmful chemicals it reduces diseases and increases mental and physical health.

- Organic foods vitamins and minerals content are higher than chemically treated foods. It gives the food extra flavor. Research indicates that all 21 nutrients show higher levels: Magnesium – 28% more; Vitamin C – 26% more; Iron – 20% more; phosphorous – 14% more.

- There is a reduction in water pollution, soil poisoning, death of insects and birds all due to the soil being organic. It restores the ecological system. Thus creating a healthy environment for all creatures. Organic gardening is labor intensive therefore you will release stress, lose weight and gain extra energy in a short period of time.

It is difficult to ignore the fact that organic is better. You need to realize that living an organic chemical free lifestyle can save and preserve the earth as well improve and extend your life. To become part of the green campaign is not that easy in the beginning; but when you start feeling healthier and get the original juicy taste of the organic fruits and vegetables there is no turning back.

5

SQUARE FOOT GARDENING

S quare foot gardening is a new gardening method. Using this   method can be highly effective when planting vegetables and herbs. If you want an easy and adaptable garden then square foot gardening is a great alternative to explore.

The garden layout is self explanatory. It is shaped in a square and depending on the size will determine the amount of plants that you are able to plant. Although you have a variety of size options you only require 62 to 64 square feet (6 to 8 sq meters) to feed a family of four.

Most square foot gardeners use raised beds. They place the beds in squares. On top of the beds a grid is placed to cordon off the squares. The beds are permanent fixtures raised above the ground. There is no digging involved. Make sure when you place the beds that the area gets a lot of sunshine. The soil mixture plays an impor-tant role. If you are not sure how to prepare the soil you are able to buy pre mixed organic soil. The soil consists out of 1/3 peat moss, 1/3 vermiculite and 1/3 compost.

Square foot gardening is an intensive gardening method that gives extraordinary results. Plant the vegetables, flowers and herbs in the squares. Keep the soil moist whilst the seeds start to grow. Do not let water drip on the plants itself to avoid plant diseases and fungus from growing. The moist soil needs to gradually dry. The best time to do this is during the day.

The nice thing about square foot gardening is that you do not need a big area to establish the garden. This makes the entire organic garden process fun for any person that does not have green fingers. Start off small and expand as you gain organic gardening knowledge and skill.

SYNERGESTIC PLANTING

Synergistic planting is an organic gardening system established by Emelia Hazelip. The entire system evolves where plants naturally fertilize the soil without intervention. The syner-gistic agriculture principles are: No chemical treatments; usage of organic or chemical fertilizers; compacting soil or cultivation are allowed.

THERE ARE a few steps to consider when you do the layout for syner-gistic planting:

- Raised beds will prevent compacting of soil due to the fact they are never trend on as well as the covering mulch prevents the rain from forming a crust.
- Use biodegradable material to create a mulch cover for example cardboard. The mulch helps to get rid of the original vegetation. Remember if you plant in the spring it is important to open up the mulch so that soil can warm up.

- Do not only plant vegetables and herbs, plant a variety of flowers throughout the garden.
- After harvesting leave the parts of plant that is not being used in the ground. Plants need to finish their life-cycle to activate the synergistic process.

Synergistic gardening is a skill that you can only learn by trial and error. If you want the gardening method to work you need to gain knowledge by doing research on the matter. The main factor to keep in mind is that the entire process needs to be natural. Let nature take its course for example if you plant onions, leeks or garlic on the side of the garden beds. They act as pest controllers.

COMPANION PLANTING

The companion planting technique is based on using certain   plants to benefit other plants by planting them next to each other. There is no need to use chemicals; because, some plants are known to act as natural pesticides. Marigold is a well known companion plant. The root of the marigold releases a natural chemical that works as an insect repellent. Legumes feed for example nitrogen into the soil; thus there is no need for fertilizers. Certain plants can hinder one another. Research shows that planting chives next to peas can prevent the peas from growing.

There are various types of companion planting. Nurse cropping for example is where tall plants are used to protect smaller more vulnerable plants. The taller plants provide windbreaks or shade to the other plants. Beneficial habitat also known as refugia is another companion gardening method. The focus is to create a symbiotic environment for insects, arthropods and other parasites that helps to control pesticides.

INCLUDED ARE few plants that are compatible with each other:

- Asparagus – Parsley, basil and tomato
- Beans – Strawberry, carrots, cucumber, celery and potatoes
- Carrots – Sage, peas, radish and rosemary.
- Dill - onions

Starting a companion garden requires knowledge. You need to be able to understand the compatibility between the plants. Use the internet as a tool to find compatibility lists. As soon as you get the hang of companion gardening you will want to learn more and experiment to see if it truly works.

VEGAN GARDENING

Vegan gardening is not just vegetables. Products that are used in the garden exempt animal products. The compost consists out of mulching, plant manures, rotating crops etcetera. Vegan organic gardening is a combination of companion and synergistic planting. The unique difference between other gardens and a vegan garden is that the fertilizers do not contain blood, bone or anything that consists out of animal debris. Popular vegan fertilizers are wood ash, seaweed and organic compost.

The soil is treated with natural substances; for example lime, reduces acidity in the soil it also adds calcium and magnesium. Neem is a tree that is used as a pest repellent. Epsoms salts are a great magnesium source. Not only does the vegan technique aid with living healthy it also helps to eliminate transmittable and bacterial diseases.

Certain standards are set by the Vegan-organic network. The reasons for the standards are to give home gardeners a guideline to follow and to control commercial gardening. The goal of vegan gardening is to feed the soil with products that do not contain harmful substances and in return the organic soil feeds the plants. If you want to conform to vegan organic gardening there is one main thing that you must remember. No animal products. You need to create an organic, natural and ecological friendly environment without using animal products.

Start off by creating your own green compost. Do research to get ideas what you can use to replace harmful methods. To be successful you need to think and act as a vegan otherwise you can disregard the entire gardening technique.

WILDLIFE GARDENING

To take organic gardening to the next level why not try wildlife gardening. Similar to synergistic planting the only extra is to create an environment to lure wildlife for example birds, squirrels etcetera. The aim is to create a small nature reserve in your garden by using plants wisely.

A plus about wildlife gardening is that is does not cost a lot of money. Look at the plants around your countryside to determine what type of vegetation grows. Create the same type of gardening scenario to stay true to the area. The closer you get to creating a similar environment the greater the chances are that wildlife will move in.

Variety is important when you are planning the garden. Think of the different types of species and the surroundings they live in. Estab-lish a haven retreat that consists out water streams, trees, flowers and herbs to make the creatures feel at home. Weeds for a normal garden will not be tolerated but with a wildlife garden it forms part of the beauty of nature.

Another important factor to keep in mind is that the garden needs to be user friendly. The possibility of making a small section of the garden wildlife can arise. You need to establish if you will be using the garden as a retreat to get away from everything or if you want to use the garden for practical purposes like for example vegetable garden.

Finding the right balance between yourself and nature can be a challenge. Giving back to the environment and preserving wildlife can be very rewarding. Wildlife gardening brings a level of peace and satisfaction. You realize your purpose on earth by feeling part of conservation.

10

ORGANIC GARDENING MAINTENANCE

Maintaining an organic garden is essential. The effort and the time you put in to establish a healthy ecological garden requires care and attention. If you look after the garden on a daily basis there is no need using harsh pesticides later on. If you want you organic garden to flourish it is up to you to keep it in shape. By trimming and slimming it on a continuous basis can prevent major gardening problems later on. There are a variety of tasks that you can implement to maintain your garden.

<u>MONTHLY TASKS</u>:

- Throw mulch in the vegetable garden at least once a month.
- Check plants and crops for any pesticides or diseases on a weekly basis. Use organic solutions to treat any infected plants.
- Make sure the ph level is correct by checking it every 2 weeks.

- Water the garden with an inch of water once a week. Keep the soil moist.
- Mow the lawn to stop weeds from growing and to cool down the soil.

Long term tasks:

- Install shades to protect lettuce and other crops to help them with the growth process. Harvest crops on a regularly basis to keep the process going. Plant a new batch of vegetables according to seasonal instructions.
- Spray your fruit trees on a regular basis with seaweed extract to aid them withstanding the heat.

11

____

POLLINATION AND GARDENING

Creating an organic garden requires all aspects of the eco   system. Pollination plays an imperative role to support the growth of plants and attract wildlife, birds, bees, and insects. To use pollination effectively you need to use plants that are colorful. Modern gardens use stone and hard landscaping features. This makes the garden less attractive for bees and other insects. Organic Wildlife gardening or synergistic planting is the ideal set up to support the pollination process.

THE FOLLOWING PLANTS **attract bees and other insects to aid with pollination:** Aster, Bergernia, Clematis, Echinacea, Impatiens, Tulips etcetera.

THE FOLLOWING SHRUBS ATTRACT POLLINATORS:
Hedra, Rosmarinus, Hebe, Buddleja, Euonymus, Lonicera, Rosmarinus, and Cotoneaster.

The aim is to design a garden with array of beautiful flowers and herbs. Pollination will take place and the ecosystem will be restored to its original state. Studies show that plants with taller stems that sway in the wind attracts more bees than flowers that are static and on the ground. Not many people know that bees are declining and this can lead to environmental destruction. Bees play an essential part; because they pollinate crops and garden plants.

It is up to society to take responsibility. Understanding the ecosystem and cultivating an organic gardening method will give hope to the next generation. You can start small by selecting a space that is suitable for flowers. You can even opt for pot plants. Take a selection of the above flowers and build an oasis of color and fragrance. Add water features for example birdbaths to invite the pollinators into your organic garden.

BENEFICIAL INSECTS

As all gardens there is always an infestation of some type of   pest. A great way to control the pests is to look at the food chain and find the pests predators (beneficial insects). All you need know is how to attract the beneficial insects to your garden. By doing this you cut out chemical sprays that are hazardous to your health and your surroundings.

Beneficial insects are insects that help you to grow plants natu-rally. Bees for example and other pollinators are seen as beneficial insects. In the beginning when you start attracting beneficial insects to your garden you will find that the pests increase for a short period of time. You need the beneficial insects to settle in and lay eggs to attack the pests you want to get rid of. Remember do not use toxic chemical sprays. This will only destroy the entire process of symbiosis.

There are many ways to invite beneficial insects to your garden. Build an insectary. This can be outside the normal landscaping area. Plant flowers in the insectary earlier than the other flowers in the garden. By the time the other plants are blooming the beneficial insects can be released onto the mites and aphids. Also use a variety of flowers for example tall daisies attract hover flies where as thyme attracts ground beetles. All insects drink water; thus find a place where you can put a saucer of water with rocks around it. Mulch helps ground beetles to stay moist and not dry out.

Introducing beneficial insects can take time. There is no need to treat plants with harmful fertilizers or chemicals. As soon as a balance is established the garden is self sufficient creating the best of both worlds for the enthusiastic gardener.

PEST CONTROL NATURALLY

Pest control naturally forms the basis of organic gardens. Green concerns promote these natural methods. A good combination of pest control ensures that all areas are covered. Maintaining healthy soil by treating it with healthy natural fertilizers and using beneficial insects will balance the ecosystem and nature will do the rest. If you encounter a pest that is uncontrollable you can use natural methods to balance the gardens symbiosis. You can aid the pest control naturally by mixing your own non-toxic sprays or carrying out a few natural pest control tips.

Aphids:

Plant: onions, garlic or chives to act as a repellent. Aphids are attracted to yellow flowers thus planting Nasturtiums can be used to prevent them from harming crops.

Borers:

Preventing your plants being infested with borers requires you to keep them healthy with organic fertilizers, frequent pruning and watering on a regular basis.

CUTWORMS:

Lure predators for example toads, tachnid flies etcetera to control or eliminate cutworms.

As a gardener sometimes you might feel using a pesticide spray is easier than getting the right plant or luring beneficial insects. That is understandable you need to focus on the bigger picture. The environ-ment is slowly deteriorating and it took many years to destroy it with toxic chemicals. Start slowly and carry out the various methods as you learn. Use technology to guide you on how to control pest naturally.

∼

INTEGRATED PEST MANAGEMENT

ntegrated pest management (IPM) optimizes the usage of natural pest control options. IPM is designed to support healthy plant growth with the minimal disruption to the ecosystem. Countries worldwide encourage the IPM program; because it protects the earth's reserves as well as civilization. The IPM concept is not only used for gardening purposes. Many industrial and commercial businesses apply the IPM program to create a healthy friendly environment.

As a gardener you need to strategies how to control pests. Putting a strategy in place forms the entire integrated pest management program. Applying natural pest control methods without impacting on the environment will ensure that the IPM program is carried out correctly. Integrated pest management is organic gardening. The same rules apply and the same outcome applies. The goal is to replenish the soils nutrients with natural products. Standards are set to control and carry out organic methods.

To determine the standards you need to decide on when to take action in your garden for example if you see leaves deteriorating and it is one or two are you going to start spraying for diseases or are you going to leave it until a plant dies. When setting your standards also draw up a maintenance plan. Prevention and control are a good option this will set the standards as you carry out the prevention. Think of ideas that you can start doing that will not impact the envi-ronment in a negative way. Start pruning your plants. Hose off the insects from your flowers, fruit and vegetables. Use an insecticidal soap to wash of infected plants.

Remember that the things you do now will take a while before it starts working. The only way you make IPM work effectively is to maintain the standards you set.

ORGANIC PEST CONTROL RECIPES

Organic pest control recipes are easy to find and easy to mix. Most of the organic material you have in your own kitchen. All you need to do is concoct the recipe and spray. Be aware that there is a difference between organic and non-toxic. Included are a few recipes that you can try on your plants.

INSECT REPELLENT MIXTURE:

4 x cloves of garlic; 1 x table spoon dishwashing liquid; 2 x table-spoons vegetable oil; 2 x cups of water. Crush the garlic cloves, add the oil and water and let it soak for 24 hours. Strain the mixture the next day and add the liquid soap. Pour mixture in a spray bottle and spray on plants.

FUNGUS AND MILDEW MIXTURE:

1 x table spoon baking soda; 1 x liter water; and 1 x table spoon soap flakes. Boil water and add baking soda. Dissolve and add the soap flakes to the mixture. Remove the leaves that are infected. Spray the entire plant with the mixture.

. .   .

TRAPS for fungus gnats and whiteflies:

4 x 8 cardboard; 2 x table spoon Vaseline; and waterproof yellow paint. Apply the paint on both sides. After the paint dries apply the Vaseline on both sides. Take the card and hang it above the plant infested area.

To find more useful organic pest control recipes logon to the internet. Type the words organic pest control recipes. You will find a variety of websites that offer help on how to get rid of pests naturally. The nice thing is that most of the products are things that you have in your home. Stop the pests from ruining your garden start spraying.

∼

16

COMPOSTING AND NATURAL FERTILIZER

Composting and natural fertilizer is the back bone of organic gardening. It is not difficult to make your own compost. You require a shovel, a designated area for the compost pile, and waste from the garden and kitchen. Start off by throwing cut grass, racked leaves and food waste from the kitchen on the pile. You throw the organic material on the pile as soon as you have the waste available. Every week you need to rake the pile of waste to speed the process up.

As soon as the organic waste material is a dark rich soil then the compost is ready to use. You need to smell to make sure the compost is in a good condition. You will find that the compost will smell bad if it is to wet or there is a shortage of oxygen. A great way to reduce the smell is to use coffee waste.

Do not use animal fats and diseased plants. Good organic products that you can use for the compost pile are wood material, waste, leaves, grass etcetera. Stay away from animal bone, manure, blood meal etcetera. The main reason for using organic fertilizer is to increase the soils quality. Using organic compost increases the nutrients in fruits and vegetables. Flowers and crops also benefit from organic fertilizer due to it being the richness of the soil.

There are alternative options that you can apply in your garden that adds the same value as compost. Watering your plants when they are dry will help the plant to draw the nutrients up into the roots. Turn the soil now and again to give it oxygen. Remember if you feed the soil your plants, fruits and vegetables will flourish.

17

MANAGING WEEDS

Managing weeds in a way that does not harm the soil, insects, plants etcetera requires knowledge, skill and perseverance. There are different types of weeds and you need to be able to recognize the weeds that are harmful.

You can apply basic easy to manage methods to control weeds. Cover bare soil with three layers of wooden mulch this will prevent the weeds from sprouting in the soil making it easy to pull out. You can put layers of newspaper underneath the mulch if you are not going to plant anything in a specified area. Water the beds and surrounding areas for at least 24 hours before weeding. Afterwards pull out the weeds with their roots to stop them from regenerating.

Try to get rid of weeds when they are small. Do weeding at least once a week and use a garden hoe to clear the smaller weeds. If you have an excessive amount of weeds on your lawn or in a specific area smother them with cardboard. Cut the grass then place the card-board on top. Wet the lawn down and after a few weeks you can replace the grass.

Be careful not to overdo the weeding process. Some weeds are beneficial for the gardens ecosystem. Clover for example improves the soil and dandelions are edible. Some weeds nectar acts as a source for pollinators. The key is to know which weeds contribute to the gardens ecological existence.

The measures that you put in place to manage the weeds in your garden is determined by the type of organic garden you have. A wildlife garden requires less weed management and a vegetable garden more. Controlling weeds in the garden must be part of your weekly gardening routine. There is no need to make the techniques complicated keep things simple.

SEED SWAPPING

Seed swapping is the latest gardening craze. Many gardeners end up with extra seeds after every season. Events are arranged where gardeners come together and swap seeds. It is a great opportunity to meet other organic gardeners and discuss planting methods that work. A person can also do seed swapping online via email or via various websites.

Adding additional plants to your garden has never been easier. Seed swapping is free and if you are seeking a rare plant chances are that swapping will help you find it. Exchanging seeds also preserves the genes and ensures a variety of plants that are strong.

There are a few things to remember when exchanging seeds online. Most websites are local based due to import and export laws. You can not exchange worldwide. People that trade seeds are fellow gardeners do not get upset if they can not help with a seed. They do seed swapping as a hobby and not as a job.

It is easy to organize your own seed swapping event. Start in your neighborhood get the people who love gardening to partake. Keep it small in the beginning. Arrange the event in someone's garden to create atmosphere and promote the goal. Ask the local newspaper to publicize the event. You can also ask the library to put up an advertisement. Get a guest speaker that is an expert in the field to talk about gardening methods. Ask your local nursery to contribute seeds to motivate the other people to bring seeds. At the event hand out pamphlets with viable information like for example what to plant when, how to prepare the soil etcetera.

As a gardener you can grow and learn with other members. Do it for free make seed swapping a fun adventure. Enjoy the experience.

19

SUSTAINABILITY AND YOUR ORGANIC GARDEN

The recent chapters explained the different types of organic gardens and it also gave information regarding how to control pests, manage weeds, mix your own fertilizer and organic pest control sprays. It is up to you to use the information and make it work. You need to establish a garden that is easy to sustain. The only way you can do this is to carry out what you learn. You need to believe in the cause and that is to restore the soils balance and to produce healthy non-toxic food.

Taking the first step to plant an organic garden is already part of the sustaining process. Stay true to the process. It is no use you only apply a portion of the process because to balance the ecosystem requires every aspect to make it work. The nice thing about an organic garden is that as soon as you reach the point that the garden is a well balanced ecological environment then to sustain it is easy. Organic gardens can flourish on its own if you add the right ingredi-ents to it.

Restore that energy of the earth. Remember your children are the future. You need to teach them your skills and knowledge so that they can carry out your quest. As a community giving back to nature and preventing further harm can make a huge difference in the long run.

There are a few things to sustain your garden. You need to make sure that you do not use any toxic chemicals, sprays or products when you fertilize the soil and spray the plants. Everything is natural and the goal of the exercise to produce healthy food from the plants by restoring the soil for future generations. Start now, become part of the green parade.